SOUL SHADOWS: TEEN POEMS IN THE DARK

Sean Blumenfeld

ISBN-13: 979-8-9905047-0-7

Part One

Introduction

Preface

Throughout my adolescent and young adult life, I have noticed people around me struggling with depression, anxiety, and other mental health issues. After doing a lot of research, I noticed that there are a lot of books about how to deal with these emotions, but not many expressing that these teens and young adults are not alone. Soul Shadows: Teen Poems in the Dark focuses on just that. This book provides relatable quotes and relatable poems I hope those who struggle with these issues can relate to and can feel less alone.

About the Author

Hi, my name is Sean. For most of my adolescent and young adult life, just walking around and observing, seeing on social media, and working in a mental health facility, I noticed that many people struggle with mental health. Two common answers were heard when asked about how they feel physically and mentally. The first answer was that they felt alone and isolated, and the second was that they felt trapped and could not escape. Being a young adult now and wanting to pursue counseling, I got to thinking that I see everywhere books about dealing with depression or how to tame anxiety, but not a book sharing creative works expressing the feelings of those who struggle with mental health. Throughout my late adolescent years and my young adult life, I struggled with depression and anxiety. It was not until late into my academic career that I found my talent with creative writing, so I wondered, what if I developed my creative writing into a book aimed to help those who struggle with feeling like they are alone in their struggles. That is the essence of this book. The book contains quotes and poems that I came up with aimed not at explaining the struggles, but at showing that you are indeed not alone in how you feel. I know I feel alone with my struggles at times and I am certain that many people feel exactly how I do. My hope is this book brings comfort to many people struggling with mental health, but if even one person can feel warmth knowing they are not alone in their thoughts and feelings, I will be delighted.

Disclaimer

This book is not meant for any official diagnosis, see medical professionals for that. This is simply a book of quotes and poems that is meant to bring comfort to anyone struggling with mental health so they feel seen and less alone. This book covers sensitive topics like depression, anxiety, suicide, etc. If you are uncomfortable with any of these topics, please feel free to skip over them.

Part Two

Quotes and Poetry

A We and a Me

About Loss

A We and a Me is a poem about watching a beautiful life end. Specifically, watching my grandmother decline until their death and being left only with the memories of her. For me the memory I was left with was my first and last knitting lesson. This is both one of my strongest memories and my last memory of my grandmother. This poem talks about the "we" in the sense that we used to do things together, but after the persons death it is no longer considered a "we" all that's left is a "me".

In the garden we lay

The time goes by fast

The best time was in the day

But even the day will not last

When day ends

A darkness absorbs light

Time seems to bend

Through the night

In the dark

A we can become a me

Which makes an arc

What was two, becomes a plea

Even light must end

One can plea

But darkness doesn't bend

A we becomes a me

All a me can do is recite

How we used to sit

It used to so bright

As we would knit

As a we closed on an end

The we couldn't remember the me

As if the mind wouldn't lend

The me of the we became absentee

Quote 1

Someone dying, leaving you, blocking you.
Is not the worst pain.
True pain is when
The darkness manipulates you and wins

Quote 2

Relationships end the moment
Both people see the inner darkness of each other
And realize their lights cannot pierce
The darkness

Quote 3

When you go from "snapping" and talking daily
To not at all,
It feels as if a piece of you goes missing

Quote 4

No matter who leaves you.
You are still strong. And, at
some point someone will fill
the void

Quote 5

Saying goodbye is hard
Because the light making you happy
Is finally put out

Cold as Ice

About Depression & Despair

Cold as Ice is a poem about the struggles of despair and depression. More often than not, depression can make someone feel mentally cold. The events throughout life: loss, grief, rejection, among so many can take away the warmth within ourselves and leave a cold shell.

Walking through a world

One sees everything

He sees birth

He sees death

He sees life

As one walks

At times it freezes

The world grows cold

Despair grows colder

Energy lowers

The will to fight dissipates

Hope gone

Happiness left

Family, whose love is gone

Family, to which one is burdening

These feelings drain

The energy, will, hope, and happiness

One must stop

His body numb

One growing ever colder

He is cold as ice

Quote 6

Some people who see the darkness choose to help it or join it
That is how nice and mean people are made

Quote 7

Life sometimes deals a
Cold hand to you
However, it takes only one person or event
To change a two to a king

Quote 8

Everyone has light and darkness within them,
It is up to you where you live

Quote 9

You know what is sad?
When you realize that you probably will never bring home a boyfriend or girlfriend
for Christmas

The Void

About Depression & Anxiety

The Void is a poem targeting depression and anxiety, similar to *Cold as Ice,* this poem metaphorically relates to the feeling of being trapped in a void. Similar to a void you see on a TV show or in a movie, voids are often dark and meant to pull you deeper inside. This poem highlights the feeling of being dragged into a deep darkness.

Alone... Cold... Dark

Curled in a ball

A boy sits

The void consumes

Deep in the cold darkness

The isolation, the depression

The boy tries to warm

He sits cold and alone

The darkness swallows

The thoughts deep

The worthlessness

The hopelessness

No matter how hard the fight

The darkness envelopes

The boy can't win

Everything is too strong

The boy tries

***

But the darkness wins

The boy wants to end himself

In this cold, dark void alone

Quote 10

When you been in darkness so long
That it feels normal,
That is when your already gone

Quote 11

Those who win against darkness are scary,
Those who learn to make it home are truly dangerous

Quote 12

Even in the darkness,
It takes one source of
Light to save you

Quote 13

Typically, those with unstable thinking
Or unstable relationships
Typically have at least one trauma point
That can be found in their past

Numb

About Numbness

Numb is a poem about the mind and emotional numbness experienced in depression. Depression is characterized by intense sadness accompanied with feelings of worthlessness and hopelessness. These three characteristics will eventually make your mind and body numb as your body stops trying to fight these feelings.

Empty, anxious, over thinking

Nothing make me happy

All that is seen is dark

The feeling of the worst

The leg starts to shake

The worst option

The "what if's" start

Every thought comes

Depression, anxiety, demons

One fights everyday

The worst form of all

Day after day

The worst I must hide

Behind a fake smile

Behind a "I'm ok"

Everyday

Quote 14

It's scary when your mind becomes so numb
that nothing makes you happy or sad,
just a neutral numbness

Quote 15

Your mentally not weak
It is your brain making you feel that way.
You are stronger than you think

Quote 16

Those who save others from darkness
Always wanted someone to
Save them, but no one did

The Bag

About the Feeling of Depression

The Bag is a poem about the feeling of depression. Depression can be described in many ways. Some will call it a void others will call it darkness. For this poem depression is described as a suffocating feeling. Similar to a void, depression and thoughts associated with depression can feel overwhelming and metaphorically suffocate you. This poem metaphorically examines the overwhelming feeling of depression and the suffocation that can be present.

Crying on the floor

One holds a bag

Crying feeling like it's over

One puts their head in the bag

* * *

One ties the bag tight

First breath is fine

Second breath is fine

Third gets harder

Four, five, six

It gets harder

One starts to struggle

Seven, eight, nine

One's vision gets blurry

Breathing fast only losing more air

Vision gets darker

One starts to fight

Scratch, scratch, scratch

One tries to tear the bag

Ten, eleven, twelve

One gets dizzy

One feels faint

One's arms go numb

One can't scratch anymore

Thirteen, fourteen, fifteen

One falls over

One is to weak

Can't breathe, can't move, numb

With one's final breath

One claws one last time

Pop

The bag opens

One can breathe

Feeling comes back

The light returns

Quote 17

There becomes a point in life when you
Tune it all out
Just stop listening
And life gets peaceful
When the peace ends it replays over and over
crying

Quote 18

The world is a never-ending cycle
Of hate and pain
Caused by humans.
Will someone ever break this cycle?

Quote 19

The world through some eyes
Is black and white
While through others is color.
For those who see color
Remember there are some that
Cannot

It is Back

Dealing with the Coming & Going of Depression

It is Back is a poem that expresses how depression can go away but also can come back. There will be times that a person will experience clinical depression that after months of treatment can go away. In the case of this poem, it examines how depression can come back even if it feels like it has gone away.

The light blocked the shadows

In this pitch dark room

Days, months of darkness

The darkness swallowed everything

Then the light appeared

***

It fought the shadows

For once

The room was bright

Ever so slowly

The light started to fade

Get dimer day by day

The darkness crept back

One strand to the left wrist

One to the right

One strand to the left foot

One to the right

One over the mouth

One covering the eyes

***

One to the chest

With the light so dimmed

The darkness takes hold

No movement

No sight

No speech

The darkness takes form

As it pulls the body below the surface

The struggle

The silence

The blindness

The light got too weak

The darkness has won

***

The body starts to suffocate

Then goes limp

The darkness is final

The darkness is complete

Quote 20

Those with kind hearts and eyes,
Have already seen the darkness
and made it their home

Quote 21

If one pillar falls
Another one will support
Until that pillar is repaired

Quote 22

Many people think of themselves
As a failure
Your not a failure
Do not listen to people
Or your brain if they
Tell you otherwise

The House

About the Darkest Side

The House is a poem examining the darkest areas of the brain and the inner most feelings of depression. This poem uses a lot of imagery as it follows you (the reader) from the surface to the darkest realms of a person with depression. This is by far my longest poem, but I feel like it serves a purpose. It is important to note everyone will have a different "house" so to speak, but this poem gives a good illustration of what someone's "house" might look like.

Sitting in a green field

On a clear blue day

The clouds were a puffy white

And the smell of fresh grass arrived

Upon staring into the field

One was able to see a parallel of the mind

In this parallel stood a house

The house was a beautiful, mellow yellow

The presence alone was tranquil

As you approach the house

A bike and a swing rest near a door

As you approach, you touch the door

The door opens as you walk inside

A bright, white hallway appears

A sense of happiness and joy fill the air

As one walks down the hallway

The sensation of being young emerges

***

One feels like a happy kid once again

When one gets close and listens hard

Part of the white on the wall turns black

Another door appears

As one approach, the happiness fades

And a feeling of dread fills the air

In a white hallway

As bright as can be

Stood a door of pure black

With a sense of sorrow emitting

Upon the opening of the door

One learns about the smile outside

***

one falls into the blackness beyond the door

The one realizes the truth about the smile

Deep into the blackness you hear sobs

It's as if a small boy is crying

One looks and searches but it's too dark

All one can hear is the sobs

It's like the boy is dead and the sound remains

You turn but begins to lose breath

It's as if the blackness is stealing the air

Your body goes numb and rigid

You fight to move and breathe

It's hopeless, you can't move

Thoughts and memories flood the mind

***

You try to resist, it's hopeless

The darkness of the mind enters your head

Betrayal of friend after friend

The loss of friend after friend

The deaths of the loved

And the harm from the blade

You scream at the thoughts fight to reach

No matter your struggle you can't move

It's like a force is pushing you back

You look and you see a boy crying

As you try to call him, you see the wounds

You see the knives, the blood, the hopelessness

You begin to feel faint

***

You lose consciousness

You awake in the hall of white

Shaking of the horror inside

In the bright hallway

Shaking from fear

Shaking from horror

One stumbles and falls

Before the floor you reach

You hand grabs a sphere

One realizes they fell into a door

A normal wooden door

One opens the door, a stair case emerges

Climbing down the stairs, it was dark

The only light emitting was from torches

***

The stairs twist and turn as one descends

One has a cool air flow upon them

A chilling air filled with darkness

A feeling of demonic powers emanate

As one descends they grow weaker

Looking at the wall one notices writing

Weak, loser, no one wants you, is read

The further one descends the more writing

Mistake, failure, disgrace, blame

One gets to the bottom sees a metal door

One last message is on the wall

Kill yourself

You touch the door and you feel a power

So dark, so sinister that one hesitates

One opens the door and almost falls

The power rushes out, it's too much

One enters anyway

A room barely lit by torch one can see

Three demons chained and a small boy

The demons have name plates on the wall

Loss, betrayal, regret

One stands and watch the demons

As they attack the boy

Blood from the small boy leaks

As he falls to the floor, to his knees

He cries and begs for it to stop

***

It's pointless

The demons don't stop attacking

It's like the boy is in a loop

Break, attack, plea, attack, break

The loop seems to be endless

You approach to try to help

The boy, bleeding everywhere, stops you

"Stay away, I don't want you to feel pain"

"I'll take it so you won't have to"

"Leave me here, you don't have to watch"

With that the boy is attacked again

His blood flying, staining your face

You walk so you don't have to watch

***

And you find the only door left

You place your hand on the knob

And close your eyes, scared of what's next

One hears the pain

With one's hand on the knob

One opens the steel door

One enters a room

It's cool as ice

Faintly lit by torches

A stone brick floor

Each step one takes

The sound echos

The sound of whimpering

Is faintly echoed

***

One reaches an opening

One trembles at the sight

A boy can be seen

Arms and legs bound

He looked like a "X"

His body dripping of blood

A black gag in his mouth

Tears falling from his eyes

Knives hanging from his body

Behind the boy, shelves of tools

Next to the boy, a man

A man with horns, who seems to chant

Loser, stabs the boy

***

Failure, stabs the boy

Worthless, stabs the boy

Waste, stabs the boy

Problem, stabs the boy

The boy whimpers from pain

As more blood drips

One yells to stop

The man turns to one

One feels his arms rise

Before one notices,

He too is an “X”

The man approaches

The boy pleads

The man ignores

* * *

The man raises a blade

And cuts one on the wrist

One screams as he bleeds

The boy crying harder

The boy shaking

One realizes the boy changed

The boy fights, useless

The boy cries as he

Watches his close friend suffer

Powerless, hopeless the boy watches

The man slashes the other wrist

One feels dizzy

One closes his eyes

* * *

One dies

The boy sobs

The man returns with his blade

The man resumes his fun

In the field one sits with the boy

One hugs the boy and says

"It's ok

No need to hide yourself behind

The smile"

The boy breaks down

Cries in one's arms

Quote 23

The worst kind of darkness
Is not being able to explain
The darkness

Quote 24

Crying is not weakness,
It is your body releasing
Pain that words cannot describe

Quote 25

There are monsters inside everyone
but those who can show others their monsters
are truly beautiful people

Quote 26

When you see a friend as a brother
Then they leave
Might as well be stabbed in the back

Quote 27

Solutions are not always
Black and white.
Solutions come in many colors

Part Three

The Light

Hope

About Hope

Up to now, we have focused on despair and the darkness around mental health. Hopefully you've gathered that you are not alone in your struggles with mental health. Few things are stronger than the darkness, like finding ways not to be alone and talking about your struggles. But there is one thing stronger than those: HOPE. The hope to emerge from the darkness, the hope to not feel alone, the hope to grow stronger. Hope is underestimated but is essential to feeling less weak in your emotions, less alone, and less hopeless.

Submerged in the darkness

One feels weak

Without hope

* * *

The darkness devours all

But one thinks to themselves

Hopes to emerge from the dark

Hopes that someone is there

Hopes someone to listen

As one begins to hope

A twinkle emerges in the void

As the hope gets stronger

The twinkle gets brighter

One feels themselves flow towards

Getting closer and closer

Before one knows

One opens their eyes

In the arms of a person

The warmth of the person

Before one knows they hear

You'll be ok, I am here for you

Out of the darkness

One strongly hoped

The light was found

One was saved from the void

Made in the USA
Columbia, SC
23 April 2025

57089469R00041